DEAR JENNY,
WE ARE ALL FIND

DEAR JENNY,
WE ARE ALL FIND

JENNY ZHANG

**OCTOPUS
BOOKS**

PORTLAND   DENVER   CHICAGO

PUBLISHED BY OCTOPUS BOOKS
www.octopusbooks.net

ISBN 978-0-9851182-0-4

SECOND PRINTING

9 8 7 6 5 4 3 2 1

Printed & bound in Portland, Oregon

Cover design by Emma Barnett

Layout design by Drew Scott Swenhaugen

Titles set in Univers

Text set in Folio

MOTHERLANDS

NEW YORK

LA FRANCE

for Michael

MOTHERLANDS

"RELISH THIS MOMENT. HOPE IT WILL COMFORT ON THIS RAINING DAY"

With no sides, I come face to face with the reproductive anxiety
later, it is known to me as the productive anxiety producing aches.
I feel achey, the swollen eyelid matching the swollen moth heads
left me feeling like the chief proponent of redundancy: as in
but you said yes but you said yes but you said yes but you said yes
or: I love you son I love you my one and only son I love you
my offspring I love you person made in my own image I love you
fetus inside me who grew up to be a beautiful young man I love you
surly thing who never smiles I love you angry young boy who lacks
compassion I love you my boy and your ability to say I hate you bad.
Suddenly, the apostle who befriended me was affixed to a doorbell
and the ringing was proof of my mother's tergiversation: she gave up
my father's wealth and created a new starvation in the western lands
that were newly zoned for the gluttons who were my friends in college.
Their funds were small and mostly hidden, when they encountered
dry mouth they wept in pain but they looked clownish with their – O –
mouths and arid faces. Cry! I told them. Cry horribly! I instructed.
It will be good to calm down. It will be good to forget the oneiric
tragedy which asks us to worry about the afterlife—here I am
as shaken as the bits of gravel that came to us from Asia. Here I am
afraid, convincing others to be the same and the self-same
guilt is as ugly as the imagination that created me, created you
created my fear of you and my wanting of you, my fear of
wanting you to cease to exist or to go on. I am too afraid
to be found out, our birthplace changed too much, so what
if I wanted to be changed, so what if I depend on summary
and quotation? I saw pickled lambs and the small horned creatures
fighting the insects who carried my grandfather to his tomb
while the rest of the city departed, the gulf was created by the embalmed

evacuation. I stand over the seas now, minor as a natural hairline

discovered suddenly after a shower, the pitiful waning:

I plan to march to the seas, I plan to make more plans

the megrims of a carefully recorded life, I will save these pages—

Don't forget me, I languish between the knots and you stay furrowed.

BURPING MY FRIEND IGOR

In bed the scissored leg is so funny
we come immediately onto wire dolls with paper eyes
that remind us of our mothers
your mother being the mother of mine
I find you intriguing and less so when my father hobbles
on the leg that wasn't blown into the western poppy fields
where you holed up one summer wanting to be a sailor
you asked if free people feel untidy
I think you think too much about freeing
souls who wriggle into the palms of my little piety
still, I need to tell you about my father
his rotted tooth in a village where everyone's names were
1, 2, 3, 4, 5, 6, 7, 8, 9, 10, 11, 12, 13, 14, 15
you come here 1 and get your brothers 2, 3, 4, 5
6, 7, 8, 9, 11, 15 to come here too
this one was too strange not to look at
my father's tooth was goo by the time anyone
finally looked at it, the dentist was anyone
he put rubber bands around my mouth
to stop me from smiling
I smiled anyway at horrible things
war and villages burning
the time my cousin 9 was lured out of the village
by the promise of candy
the next time I saw him he was a Thai tranny
and I ate pad Thai with relish
the savory filling of my insides ought to be presented
in awards swimming in split seams
I felt scammed when I saw anyone
split my father's tooth in four

the hammer was small as a broken fishbone

and the sound was so horrific

I burped vomit into my hands

feeling the tin drum inside my ear

begging to be washed like my father washed me

"You're a cat and I'm a river whose only purpose is to protect you:

when you fall in I run against my own current"

I think I am hearing all of this although each arcanum

I am allowed is as diamond rough as tightening

the skin above my father's eyelids

which falls down in sleep

keep him from seeing

the eructations which vacate my body

like the ghosts of whoever we may have once been.

LET THEM LAY THEIR BUTTERFLIES ON A POCKET-HANDKERCHIEF ON THE GRAVEL

Or I will be found and the clouded head

will purple from swelling, the burp will be fine

spreading to the Asian shores of Turkey

the Europeans are on yachts   we pass them

a summer gone by without either parent

dying; suddenly I am afraid of it—

the memory of being too old

to form a donut with my brother

my aunt my father my sister my cousin my mother

my family tree turned into a dam we blocked

all the future droplets and the lessons

and the cities along the silk road

Once in a Mongolian van the driver turned out

a serpent, his hissing tongue was thin as a stem

we climbed on the roof and waved at the toothless youth

who lost their thumbs to the same hammer

we would have wept on the tracks

as we passed the places we said we would see

before marrying and starting families

if only our families knew who we were

before we wrote down our dreams

putting pressure on reality to align as perfectly

as the veins of a leaf falling on wet cement

the concreteness of it all as amazing as the Japanese beetle

embedded in my father's palm—

the blood leaving him and I was helpless

I laid captured butterflies on his eyelids

let him see what he wanted the next time we met

I was old and he was so shriveled I sat him

next to a pebble and they became close immediately

I was envious, inconsolable   my gigantism

embarrassing and difficult to hide

I blame my jejune ancestry, the historical inevitability

the creation before the consent, the explosion

or the awareness or the maturation

were all as frightening as I had anticipated

and there was no one to report this to.

THE KUMIHO INSIDE A DUMB WAITER

I did suffer; the childhood I drew for you was only a flower I found in a lot with your car, all burnt. I picked a shard into my foot and now I walk with a limp. My mom had a friend with regular lips then she ate peppercorn fish and her lips marbleized. My brother, when he was younger, fit inside a tire and we took it for a drive. Afterwards he was a tire and in order to love him we polished him daily and remembered not to leave him out in the sun too long. My sister jumped into a fish tank, became a whale and broke the tank, then our house. We lived inside her for ten days. When we realized she forgot who she was, we were so sad that we threw bricks and tore her stomach lining. The blubber wrapped itself around my head like I was Persian. The sultans who offered me opium never bothered to look at my face, which was old and brackish under the light. My whole family was born this way and we had come to terms. One day my father will kill me and my mother will drown him in a tub on accident. It won't have mattered that just yesterday I washed my father with a sponge. His skin was mossy and wiped off easy. For months we grew potatoes, maize and pods of rice until my mother found out and eliminated dampness from the house. She was nonplussed. So was my father. He had shit himself and I was too ashamed to show him the piles of dry rags in the house. Don't I miss my brother? Don't I miss my sister? A tertiary painting is when an elephant paints an elephant on a blank canvas. Last month an elephant killed five elephants and later that same elephant was killed by one of the five elephants' cousins. I found myself so depressed that I didn't even have the strength to donate to my usual stunning array of good causes in danger of being forgotten. Going for a short ride into the country and paying to see octopi in a museum, I felt romantic and small. Today I felt nothing. Doesn't matter. Anything can be felt or not.

I SAW A SKULK

This was back when I lived on a mountaintop

It looked like a cone:

The balancing act

was more difficult than you could imagine

Who cares if only one thing is drawn to scale

(my head) (your fingers attached to my missing finger)

(the punitive wakefulness of mornings

alone) (the tiptoeing and the wandering off)

Who cares if you're smaller

than one of the periodic elements

I tried to turn into water

Later Michael taught me alchemy

I found that small as well

Later my brother changed his name to "Og!"

Before that, "Sixty cents!"

When I bought a single carrot I thought of him

I walked into a room full of bromides

They were interested in me and I thought

Of course you'd be

They were shown a slideshow of a performance

of a scripted exaggeration of a theatrical reinterpretation

of my life and who I used to be

They clapped for me, reinforcing my outline
as a shady place for entrapping the past
and the pre-past passing of years
I'm only depressed for a moment when I show them
the drawing of the mountaintop where I lived—
My father slept on a cloud
I kept the swelling down with a cane

In the mornings, I slid to the base of the mountain
fulfilled my duties as a rhapsode
denouncing all of Greek culture; "I will not reference
Aeschylus!" I said to my friends who were eating rice
and wearing rice hats and being ignorant of their
ignorant ignorance; "I will bring you the Wu's, the Lao's!"
At that point someone banged three pots together
called it Chinese; they were right and I was wrong

I shook hands with the bromides, the questionable
youth who came already as an imitation of their future:
one had wrinkles around her lips and was tired
of the way society treated her like cattle
"Mooo," I said
It's all very scientific and it's all very necessary

When I saw my father floating on cumulus clouds
the accumulation of all of these years of feeling
and not saying anything was too great
I purposefully rolled down
enduring the thorns and the branches and the bramble
and the broken glass and the upright bottles
and the beetles and the whole decay of my mountain slope

The neglect was my neglect
I didn't know what had happened and I was slow
to find out what was there
at the bottom was my grandfather's shrine
"These are turban days," I say to his portrait

You and I keep meeting at the bottom
I meet other balls of dust and together we forge a history
later, in meeting new friends, I forget all of this.

SOLECISM

"I find your aestheticism so solitary that you
must not be very happy," this seems true and untrue
to be laughing like say all day
aren't you ever sad, if not, what is there
not to be sad about, the aphoristic helping
is petty but not granular, not like searching
for you at night after five arguments
when you wear your dark hat you are
the color of the nights we fought
I thought grass was poison and ate it by the handful
it turned out to be healthy
I was blissful in the morning until I realized the cuts
on the walls and the floor we broke
in thirds like a pizza that could not be
and this was our own present
the starveling's tale was about a woman eating
cheese and throwing up, thus she was
the first woman with an eating disorder
the Victorians recoiled in horror, I swear
they strapped marrow against the nape
of someone very white and very savage
(a mongoloid/a black person/an indian
not from india/an Indian from the continent of India/
a West Indian black as night/my ancestors
pale as the first known morning) ate the neck
like it was just the jutting out extra bone
of the marrow trap I'm narrowly ensconced in
the complete rapture of the tearing of assholes
the people kind, the shitting kind
and the plugged king of wet nurses:

aka my father before he became my mother's lover

aka my grandfather before he died

and was just a thimble of ashes in a box

mass produced in gaungdong province

where he built roads and slammed his fist down

in defense of city centers with walking radii

for the goats and the children who love them

and in this box lives a box with fifty

thousand other boxes.

SWELLING

This bad back was back to show me
the bad in repeating, saying no to me
was not saying no to my family, we three
in a line, the best houses built by the Chinese
occupied by others, your other is your
self-absorption, the full headiness
absorbed through sheets of open mouths
you're open to openings like this cave
intestines tied up and worn and
now you want to have warm things.

FUNNYSHAMBLES

We are going to be symbols
or we are going to be signified
or you will end sentences with
Chinese words and I will admire them
for being so strange
the etrange was so dead giveaway-
-y
eee if you feel welcome
eee if you feel like laying on the ground
with your spread holistic judgment upon me

the shepherd and the shepherd's wife
and my grandmother's bad
ear
and her totality
and not saying hi to friends
and not editing
and not watching others
and not being a poet
and not being a lyricist
and not myth making
and not turning into a snake
who burrows into the sun
so that we may have shadows
as long as lean as beans pulled thin
until we are the stalks of light
that bisect our vision on occasion
and it's like I see the top of you
and the bottom of you
and the missing middle is just a sunbeam
wrapped around me like a water hole.

SERIOUSLY, UNLESS YOU'RE CHINESE, I WANT YOU TO FUCK

I thought of a great mansion

the fissuring streets were pressure

I had the insurance of five candied women

they were Chinese and like me told to bark

so behind the tree was carved some

They don't understand irregularities in strokes

I noticed something about being

free and young and supposedly imitable

all your friends are stark white

I ask that some of them at least learn tones

tasking a sad thing to shiver like scintillating lakes

the shivaree of my current union—

we trumpeted horns and ate every part of an animal

you cannot possibly understand—

there are no Christ references

this person has never heard of apostles

The Psalms I spelled The Palms, Last Vegas.

FIRMAMENT

Remember when we first heard about the firmament
thinking it was the firming up of life, as in one's goals
for becoming the person one knew one was meant to be
even before one was endowed with a consciousness
even before one was born, even before the universe
was endowed with a borning, even before the universe
was conscious of the universe being boring one day
I borrow your knife and carve a heart
above my heart and carry it around everywhere
underneath the cover of the boring sameness
of the universe my mother carried around in the same hand
as the one carrying around apples for when we got sick
and needed to hear the sound of quick things
all I knew were the small things you knew
I told you the same universe has bored us because
we think the universe jumps from one hot coal to the next
the dancing frogs in Spain were only a myth, our doubles
who were rich by the time they turned sixty
went to Spain and confirmed nothing
should be grieved when no one can say
what they saw the moment before their death
was the place given to them before they were born
before anything existed there were places that existed
with grass forming the green of the seas
and our cold fingers forming the blue of the firmament
when it opens up and we see how we will soon gulp down
the roads that sit on our decaying molars, our gift to an idea
that cannot exist and so we feel there is meaning to life—
we know there is and there is or else there isn't, is there?

ST. VITUS' DANCE

Once again, I became jealous, herky jerky. Inconclusive waving, then they cut down my legs. I was too small to fit in the metal box they built to stunt me. I was stunned by these dreams where she appeared as beautiful as 观音. This was when I did not know s/he was a queer. The queerness of your distance is not queer at all, as proved by the toad scared stiff by a stinging worm dangling like a Christmas ornament. We find the pleasure of the normal to be so similar to the antics of the paranormal that your para-plumes are practically the last great sky I will ever see. The puffer fish my Japanese cousin stains her teeth on gave us sugar, made us dependent on the dictatorships who were dependent on our dependence on their depending on who had glass in their veins opening them to the toxins. You're dependent on the idea that we ought to ignore jealousy because of how embarrassing it is to say, "Is she nice? You never talk about her." This, I agree with. This, I am aware of. Though I tell you it's like a flower blooming from the largest and most useful vein, you must be aware that I'm only attempting to convince myself of ancient nostrums—the low whispered lie, the printed delusion. The truth is: it's like watching the morning workmen lay concrete over where once lied tiny violets and the golden needles of my happier days.

I'M STILL

the red rimmed lake   drained   you were in clothes borrowed
from my father   his chest swelled from the chestnut we micro-
waved   the first time he tried tasting it   it exploded on his
lip   for years   my father had no lips   we put the chest-
nut back in the microwave   our memories make us cruel

we were speechless

then we were logging words   as usual   it was for my mother
you aren't my father because you didn't let me place a chestnut
on your lip   carpe diem   to seize the day   you must call
me   I wrote Patrick an email   once   he traced the bites on my
legs   that later exploded   I'm angry   so what   so's everyone

I did want you   not wanting you was not the same as you not want-
ing me   to want you   are you   you   are you you   are you   not
you   are your flowers not you   your perfect flabby stomach is flabby
and not you   the bits of chestnut were the same   as the bits of
my father   we ate from the same explosion   he is part of me now

you are not   you are notyou are not

WORD

The burning of forests

no one knew

to stop

before the trap

at the bottom

there were ghosts

I was a ghost

before I was a ghost

at the bottom

of rivers

dams

pipelines

through all of Africa

the gold coast

the opium wars of my fathers

who were born Japanese

when they baptized me

it was to prove

something

I came out of the water

a locust

then a lotus

a Chinese woman

with purple lips

the bounty

of our feet

fucked as the grassy plains

were fucked

where we cast off our toes

no one knows

who the first ghost was

no one knows

where ghosts live

no one knows

the nice ghost house

where they play chess

and throw around crackers

no one knows

the nice place you will go to

when you are ready.

FOUNDER

when did they discover you   the wheat fields infested with hay
fecal weather made this world so feeble   the whole Atlantic far-
ted   first you were crow nested   first you walked ducklegged
first the duck egg was black   first you and your goonfriends lit
up   the constellated pixel screen   why weren't you there when
we first were shown   the wagging hand   the dyed lashes   the
eyebrow scar   the angelic curl and its opposite   if my people
existed for only two thousand years   then why do I still fall off
horses   fear my children   flashy peregrine twig legs   hold-
ing me steady   I know I am supposed to be   the foundation

you were arrogant when we first met   this is normal   some men lack vital organs   surgery cannot correct that   the alchemy of person to person conversion   like the body of Christ   having lunch   with Mohammed   both penises erect   the Chinese priestess walks in with all her robes   later we realize her penis and give her some credit   my people deserve the same credit or much more   much later   we'll credit them with the birth of comedy   the invention of poetry   the first ones to feel pain   when a tree is cut down   they are the last ones to eat hamburgers   you leave a bag of french fries and surely I will eat them   before the grease hardens   my little homunculi army start running everywhere   the snakes   defenseless finally   rest for a moment she is long and deboned and cannot lift her eyes   above the tall grass   I wait for my people   to seize me   after they've written their own history   I will show them grammar and punctuation we'll feel it necessary   to live long lives   to reject our captors

if you record us   we will find your books   tear out the pages
devoted to strange oriental lives   we'll live in graves and make you
eat   the still living gizzard   the still living spleen   the heart and
the choking and the right brain   we enter and leave the circle when
we wish   and you   you contain some things   the easter parade
and the cold spring harbor   your careless ankles   swinging wildly
into my imperfect domain   where it is bitter and we demand a pen-
ance   if not that then at least a gesture that your people are sorry
cannot stand it   and will no longer loot from us   when bored

A SCIENCE

What is exfoliation?

The Orientalists came and opened up a Chinese restaurant/ all poets are humane/ I met a non-poet and spat in his face/ his sister was a lawyer/ she was dispassionate and terrifying/ once I met a pastor/ he was born without thumbs/ when we hitchhiked he pointed his cross at me and I was saved from hitching up my skirt/ later/ I had to anyway/ he pushed his ghost thumbs into my ears/ they came out like piss dribbling down my legs/ to capture it all he placed jugs underneath my spread knees/ he walked on stilts with a jug hanging from each ear/ he tattooed jugs on my face/ the locals embraced me/ my family refused acknowledgement

What is ransom?   A title which has been taken away from you and
which you did not know the details of your own
ownership until someone points it out and suddenly it
is as if you have always had too much to regret and
you say every morning, *I could have done so much
so differently.*

What is weathering?

The storm was insufficient. My mother didn't know how to write. I showed her and immediately, she wrote a poem:

A poem is only a poem when someone only obscures their feelings and asks someone else to explain and then answer to them.

That was her poem after I unscrambled it, before it was:

A answer only poem
to someone
when feelings asks
obscures their
and when
to else only a poem is then
them and explain.

What is frost action?

Most substances/ including water/ you are either composed of water or you are composed of/ ?/ what are you composed of/ ?/ I want to go fast and have you/ ask me to slow to a whimpering hush hush so slight even the curtains feel deadened inside/ I can shun the process/ I can wait for anything/ the enviable talus slopes were created so that we would trip often/ you trip often/ I wait for you to subdue

What is a novel?

I wanted to pass/ your father/ the failed poet
noticed/ *be like me* he said/ *okay* I said/ *no don't it would
be far too sad* he said/ *I won't* I said/.../

What is erosion?

We do not eat at Chinese restaurants unless owned by first or second wave Orientalists sure of their own past.

We only care about the sweet sour chicken
in Shanghai, Xianggang (Hongkong), Guangzhou
(Canton), and the shrimp in Sichuan (Szechuan), and
the beef in Hunan, Shenzhen, Xi'an, Harbin,
Heilongjiang, Wenzhou, Yunnan, and the duck in
Bejing (Peking), or the horses in Aomen (Macau), and
the rice in Yangzhou, Yunnan, Shangdong, and the
free livestock in Xizhang (Tibet), and Nanjing where
the earth was never once touched

What causes slow mass wasting?

The soil creeps/ we are a tiny bit sad/ the tiny kid in Hanzhi's science class climbed a ladder to the toilet seat/ he fell in/ the greatest fall was when I was reading the bible while walking/ while eating ice cream/ while paying attention to the people leaning out of cars/ while lifting my arms to cause a scene/ while slowing down my blinking to seem intriguing/ while noticing my age as I fell into a dazzling pit of coal/ a year later/ I still hadn't taken up any fights/ I'm still in a process of recalibration/ the recovering of my own self was difficult when faced with so many great people/ the ones who spoke well/ the ones who walked well/ the ones who moved well/ I envied every one/ who was well/ here I offer my arm to have Jane's voice/ here I offer my legs to have Anna's diction/ here I offer my neck and clavicle to have Sarah's gravity of gab/ her chatter as solemn as ceremonial wreaths/ here I offer my hands/ feet/ and knees to have Tony's superior alienation

How does human activity
affect landscape?

I'm only as lonely as these comparisons/ I
don't want to be an old stream with its ox-
bow future and its meandering pertinence/
the impertinence of this decay/ this topsoil/
this rounded tear drop of ice is my till/ this is
the pulpit from whence you showed me the
ranting eye and the scary smile/ sustaining
nothing/ these are buildings for trucks to take
a gift you buy me in Tucson all the way to
Antwerp/ where the old masters don't care if
you show respect or if you rip a tree from the
tidy storm they were commissioned to paint/
I did go back in time to uproot those leaves of
grass/ to throw them in Walden's pond/ to
oppose slavery so completely/ is just as
impressive as doing anything/ I tripped over
Pushkin and made him apologize/ *Apologize!*
Apologize! Say sorry!/ Sorry he said/ *No problem* I
replied/ he laid back down/ blocking all
possible paths.

NEW YORK

THE FIRST FANCY FEAST OF FANCY

In Lisbon you watch spiders become nudists
and I become a nudist as openly
as your wanton need for reproduction
to be arbitrary, and it is.
Look at me, my existence
improved nothing, the world
still gasped when the president
revealed his asscrack
the smoothness of a child
who has been sandpapered
into a blister which we pop
by running in bad tennis shoes
on the courts of ancient history
where my people put a pile of bricks
on an island and Korea was born
later, the Korean war was where
my grandfather's arms vanished
the false note of us
standing with streaming tears
in front of the Holocaust memorial
was played over loudspeakers
which hung like ripened fruit
in the backyards of every important person
like my sister's accountant
and your mother's doctor's secretary's gardener
who is my sister's accountant's sister.
Other people have sisters? Yes, and whales
have noses and missing teeth
can grow in size if you leave them in milk
which is why when I open my mouth

you think what you see is a cavern

where our babies become feral

the marks in trees you think

some kid carved with a knife

but here I am beaming head to toe

showing my invisible teeth, my future

wreath which tells me I am a friend

of spiders and their genitals

which fip flap like a bell made of flesh

which hangs between my fingers

as I grab hold of my friends, my people

the ones who woke me when I was sinking

and on the verge of a colossal disappearance

from this flawed, frangible world.

If anyone was to see me, I hope they only notice:

"A thousand coruscating shafts of sunlight…

… illuminating nothing."

BACCHANAL

…but remember
you brought me in a car that resembled a box
it was a box we called by its impossible name
it is impossible to take our organs
and connect them on a string
like when we lived next door to a woman
who forgot who she was and made a clothesline
from her flesh when we saw her
she was just raw pink ooze

At the sweat
you said you were not going to show yourself
me either but then there was a moment
when you spoke of your brother
and I learned that my mother
was not really my mother
the holy spirit is the time you wore my clothes
and spent time with my friends

In the evening I had no self to recover
and I became small enough to exist
in the pores of seagulls
what I had hoped to find
could not compare to what I think I saw:
the tops of all the cities we were born in
destroyed and unrecognizable
brick and clay and mud roofs
as mangled as a trampled field
The wildebeests were perched
on my childhood home

I saw my grandfather's face

clawed in fourths

instead of saving him I saved myself

useless though in the dark

of the sweat I did not feel anything

my skin bursting open like an arrow

pointing in every direction I extended myself

intending to become as round as a wheel

with infinite spokes and nothing to bound it closed

IT'S LIKE A MECCA FOR THESE LITTLE THINGS

In the dawn night, I'm afraid to look at myself. When they die, little knives sprout out of their shells. Stepping on one after getting into an argument with you about corn and how it has destroyed our extended families, I felt myself being quartered into thirds and eighths and ninths and twelfths, but if these little things are my children the way you and my brother are God's children, then I should feel something deeper than I do when I wake up and see a hundred of them falling down from the ceiling-top all at once like a dark red sheet coming down to asphyxiate us—the little spots just brilliant circular visions. We did not know what was coming for us and we heaved in a row like the tall grass that grows on water when the breeze is uniform like wet tin this din is all there is. I'm seeing small deaths, minor accidents, tiny scars and not stirring at all.

GLUING SPRINKLES ON MY HANGBAGS

Though I am leaving in two days, though there are spoons in the house that are too big for even a broken mouth, though the hanging fork was so blunt my eyes felt washed walking underneath a paper moon I made in France for you while you were in Lisbon reading French newspapers and thinking of riots that started in Lisbon where I first lost my self-esteem to a man who wanted to fuck me and that was a first. In the doorway you lick my face and arms and both of us are unimpressed by my cunt but you slobber over it and I think ? ? for a quick moment you are ? ? ? for a second we act like ? ? ? ? for a minute while you are slobbering we both consider ? ? ? ? ? ? while I am thinking about ? ? ? ? and also ? ? ? in the meantime I fear you think I'm ? ? ? and I wish you were ? ? ? ? ? ? ? ? ? ? ? ? You shake tiny non-pareils over me. You rainbow ring my areoles and I lay before you like an ice lake. When you lick me again you rip your tongue and the confetti sprays in every direction.

DANGGGGG

Where are you/ are you driving in a car/ thinking about not-me/ the hoarseness of anxiety rubs at the ventricles in my heart/ I ventilated the house/ matriculated through the star/ beneath the ideal of what-evs/ I stopped for gas/ your gaseous head is how you so quickly destroyed me/ though I am the last of the Chinese Argonauts/ though I am/ someone/ someone/ tried to argue/ I could not have been/ anyone/ I said why/ ??/ Have I a Mongol's face/ ???/ Someone is not from a long line of Grecian alchemists/ (he said: I will turn your heart into gold/ I said: how will you turn stone into gold/ he said: how will the planet spin from left to right if your mind is as indivisible as a kiwi seed/ we turned it over in my mouth/s/ to make sure it was a difficult thing to chew/ now I know that alchemy is not simply the study of turning things into gold/ if you contract meningitis and spend thirty days and thirty nights turning over in golden fever/ you will contract visions/ without having to ask/ the vision of the world/ opened into your cavities/ before you concaved and became inexistent/ go on)/ Someone said/ let's not turn this into an argument/ too late/ ?????

THE WORST DAY, NOW I'M
GOING TO KICK SOMETHING

Michael: the children are safe, the good looking ones

the apple cheeked ones and the pearskinned ones

and the plum lipped ones and the orangeteethed ones

and the muscat ribbed ones and the pineapple wristed ones

and the boysenberry pupiled ones and the kiwi-eared ones

and the durianfooted ones will not be harmed—

if they are, it was your father, the culprit.

      The absent one

we found in a basement full of dappled matches.

The thaumaturgical restraint was lovely for a second

then we were sick of it and reverted to the material world

we grew up with the susurrus promise of all known things

presented itself unobscured, hummed in our little hearts

made us seem more than we were, though this

we only found out later.

WHEN MICHAEL GETS HERE
I'LL TEACH HIM MAHJONG

Poring over the last five cuntrags

lined up in a row telling me

your style is just temporary—

the flare ups, the osteopenian guilt

mammoth and insurmountable

my anger was shingles

the shiver you felt was a bad one

my voice warped by the spineless stents

which gave me every disease

the unhappy premature stench of tinnitus

the titties of morning

committees that succeed in spite of

carpe diem written to exacerbate

my carpal tunnel, my hydronephrosis

and the impetigo of every cloud

this is less about me and more

about the pleasure of scraps

found words and the rejected moments

were herded to a field where I stand

with a bouquet of stems to eat

until I puke and the weird bunnies are all me

sad not to be with you until June.

LIFESTYLE: I THINK I HAD A NICE LIFE AND THEN I WAS DOING WEIRD THINGS LIKE TALKING ABOUT HAVING A BAD LIFE.

Someone with a bad life said they were having a good life

I believed them

what's not to believe about things that are said

I said, This is just to say I'm saying

john keats was married to vladimir nabakov

they gave birth to my aunt who spoke no Spanish

and colonized all of western Europe

and that's why michael's dad ate my left toe leaving me

crippppled

YOUR POOR MOTHER IS PORCINE

your poor mother is porcine

I swear she ate the porcini mushrooms raw

and I just about died

when she slopped around

I watched her and said

gawd that lady needs sum

manners or some

good hard je ne sais quo

YA DONE CUNT

she doesn't like the way you write

it's pretentious

yah

I know it is

that was her talking as you

Yah, she's annoying

that was me talking as me

about her

BEING JEALOUS FOR THE FIRST TIME TODAY
SINCE I WOKE UP ONE MILLISECOND AGO

The pink nailpolish unchipped tells me

I'm not sorry enough

for making your life not as good

for not knowing how to create a letterpress

I press your head between several anchors

the result is a feature length

I sleep at 3 though I tell vauhini to leave at 10

the night before I sleep before it's dark

and wake up in the dark

it's two days later

who the heck are these

little punctuation marks

to say

ha ha

ha ha

my humor is good

this is a poet's poem

written by a degenerate

illiterate

literal

piece of crap.

MICHAEL

We find you strange

this wire of weird hanging ass-out

the fiery cleavage, the eternal spotlight

of a sunset line of weirdness inside me

weirding out your mother

who was always weirder than my mother

who was as weird as the first chinese person

to say his name was chinga and the rapper

Chingy took that and made a song

about his dick that my kids memorized

for school where I teach old people yoga

to cope with the end of life

the cessation of things for example

I noticed your thing hanging out

was a nice touch to this thing

we think is a thing between us

and it is, in fact, so.

to give myself syndromes

to give carp to your seashore

foamy seamen on seahorses are on the rise

but their sperm count

is a depressed thing

this is a depressed thing

standing for hours

in the same depression

your anys are my boxes

my nourses are nursing you

this nurse is a sample nurse

this muse is a sample muse

the garden where the uni grow

have no peace of mind

or thoughts of hairy bung-cold lunges

the luncheon was a disaster

as was the plunging of your fisted anus

into water where it was cool

and not worried about weird fingers

tickling you and your icicle heart

is just a heart

these diarrhea chips

won't shut you up

you take popsicles into your knuckles

like rings attached to the doorbells

that wake up my father

he sleeps so little

you are too selfish to think

of the importance of that

as equated with blake

who is equal to homer

who is equal to the whole

equation of homoeroticism

you've been in an accident?

I will sew your eyeballs back into their sockets

when they pop out

I will hide the children

in my layers of skirts

this is the job of a chinese seamstress

you find me chinky and very fun

this chinny life is all

you're chiming about

you're my mother's mother

come embrace thee and be good

for once.

THE MOST BORING PEOPLE WHO THINK
THEY ARE THE MOST IMPORTANT PEOPLE

If only you had grown up

to be a gerontologist

you could have diagnosed yourself

the kershuffle

I'm shuffled into the wrong category

if you think bibimbop is the soon tofu

to my mother's loose chink vagina lips

you are right

to notice the bad smell

was my period

I fling blood clots from my vagina

I find you striking

at the little dim lights

you're kind of a deer

in summer in clogs

and the stomping sounds you make

across the first kitchen counter

my father ever sanded

bring me to tears

I tear up

the first love letter

your mother saved

the moment

when you could have become a politico

but you choose to wag your smelly rag

this semen balloon floats

above your head

because you seem boring

and others critique you

when you talk about greatness

I think I am great

because I see

my grandmother's blood vessels

when I lay down in the tall grass

and from that point on

I am so alone

even the trees pity me

when they lose their limbs.

PLUSSA

I waited too ong so the long wang was stupid

I was going to write about Michael's semen

small phrases that will show up here and also in his poems

I WILL CHASE YOU UNTIL YOU ARE SHY

vous est entretuer

don't die [Chinese words]

the poem thrown against the wall comes back

smaller than my baby fist

my first words: semen is on the chair;

I was born there;

I also died there; my small grave is also here; it's 5;

I should not be thinking

of graves or sleeplessness or

mornings when I might not wake up

too nicely.

I THOUGHT YOU WERE
COMING BACK TO APOLOGIZE

Lies are lies, you said. Not lies are lies. I'm not a lie, I tried to write on the wall but the pen slipped through my fingers and had a life of its own, full of neglected sorrow, you were no longer there but I felt the presence of you telling me it was a lie, these ideas, this idea that each dream will not infinitely unfold into another dream and each nightmare just a coil inside the spiral of another nightmare that might grow into a human being. If I stay myself then I'll not care what I understand. I ate a hundred pies to forget about you and when I finally exploded, the bits of me were being tossed into places as magnificent as the Dead Sea and the Salt Lake in the winter, when salt grows as tall as redwoods, toppling onto a person or two and scrubbing them of the facsimile sheen we grew over ourselves, if not for protection, then just for the fun of it.

YOU GO AWAY FOR A MONTH
AND COME BACK A GADABOUT

me I stay a cynic

later becoming a stoic

later my friends point out I'm neither

you're a zen Buddhist, they say

and your skin has the texture of rice

oh right

my name is the sound of three pots clanging

against a tin garbage can

my family is related to lao tze

and my mother taught me filial piety

my cunt grows sideways

when a man wants to fuck

he gets at a right angle

a yi ayi a ya a ya a yaaaaaaaaaaaaaaaaaaa

and it's over.

I ATE MARIGOLDS

I ate Marigolds   for attention   no one noticed
I was forced   to go public   people watching   themselves as long-
er limbed creatures   they have   um   no beauty

I DO WANT TO RECOVER

But I do want to recover/ the shock/ of going to the bathroom/ thinking gentle thoughts later/ sudden-later/ I'm shitting black coils that pile/ my ass warms the warmth/ warmed by shit coils/ you advise me not to be coarse/ in calling the ass a "butt"/ or the butt a "hole"/ or the hole a "dungheap"/ or the dungheap a "turd dumping ground"/ or a turd dumping ground a "place where shit comes out of"/ or a place where shit comes out of a "tight opening for hard and soft stools to blast out"/ or a tight opening for hard and soft stools to blast out an "other birth canal where going into labor means giving birth to a shitbaby"/ I truly want to say to you/ SHIT baby/ or how about you come back now and we'll rake unhappiness/ from each other's backs/ like the leaves that never disappear in winter/ and I'll stop/ I would rather you choke me/ you would rather you choke me/ I heard you asking the bath salts if I've ever cried selflessly/ I bring up the time I was so constipated I cried at the exertion/ like how pulling off each leach takes a drop of blood/ and you had said/ See / ????/

THE TEORAMA'S OF SPAIN

I mean the corteges, I mean the corsages
I mean the courage and the core lodge
where you hung your coat, removing links
to make everything super duper
this body odor is super duper
and this body is super duper
no one person has learned my language
I continue to learn everyone's language
take cruises with different types of people
to learn the Jamesonian default of nostalgia
the simulacrum where you finally had courage
to tell your mother you love her a lot—
you penisblowing piece of crap!

TEENY TINY

I guess I just want to take no time
reading her poetry. Its very good, you said
to study seriously. I noticed the patterns
in one second. What could you tell me
that would shame me into attention—
for what took a life was not important.
What's important is this is not how
I want to spend my life. The time we have left
is enough for two claps while listening to James Brown
fall on his dead leg. I have a dead head too
and a dead egg. We ignore the scallop-pinot
who changed poetry. Being not-poets is not
too facilitating, though I am fazed, in fact.

IF NO ONE IS LOOKING AT ME
I WON'T BOTHER TO READ KAFKA

It's to seem very smart, the book in my hands

is Betty and Veronica, Archie and Pals

a smut novel about a monkey

who jams his cock inside a woman

who is an identical twin who fucks

her own twin in front of their brother

who jerks off into a cup

his mother drinks in the morning

who pisses on their dog who knots

his wiener into a hard-on

who gives blow jobs to their ponies

who I ride into the evenings of my dreams—

you are usually there and the star spackled sky

is usually just the hand of my mother

extending over the celestial boom of boom-booms—

the Brazilian ass, the pussy-pussy, the Hungarian kiss

the hungering stare, the limber lumbering

of all the clunkers like the time you wore a dress

to show me how at ease you were

with my femininity and the stapled

tampon with dried blood clots was indeed

nice to touch when your face was rounder

and there was love all around

WHAT IS A PAPER MOON
AND WHAT IS A PEPPER MOON?

I live in a pepper room

cut outs

of your last hermetic hug were strung

like rubies

your fingers were on the floor

crawling

towards my diamond bunghole

escaping

with a little bag on a stick

some strangers

remarked 'don't get why life's so hard for that asshole,'

there's a lot not to get.

BRUNO BRUNO BRUNO

When I was a child I lived in a house that lived inside a house

how that house was a child and I had to pet it so

petting it was liking it was like petting it as a child

the house was housely and I was a house child

who needed taming like the house and the peeling paint

needed a child to lick the dead arsenic catnip

left by the peeling paint of the house inside my house

and this house of bruno bruno bruno was weakened

by street kids and a hundred chamberpots all filled

I notice you walk in the door fainting

as in you are fainting your way through the day

and in the door I am there that dream

that last wayward dream pushing knots through your legs

so that you might be strong not just straaaaa a a a aaaaaaa

straaaaa means I love you come back to me or I die

and a a a aaaaaaa means ahhhhhhhh the day

LA FRANCE

COMEFARTS

I show you my virtue when I come farting

and fiscal responsibility has the same verdure as some ventures

you play like a donkey with six legs

each leg clasped to a tree

and we drag a forest through the forest finally

you are farting

compare the time I shat my pants at the library

because I could not be bothered to stop reading

I was wet from the non-solids I excreted

I was wet from the rain that followed me into caves

I was wet because I was wet

I was wet and you asked to touch it

I was wet and you didn't notice it on your leg

I was wet and I sat on fine china

I was wet and I was born in China

I was wet and a horse kicked me in the face

I was wet and in my dreams I was wet

I was wet and asked a stranger to jerk off onto my face

I was wet and I hurt my back trying to reach

I was wet and I farted dead sperm from a butthole that doesn't want to poop

Except in libraries

Except in bus shelters

Except on my neighbor's lawn

Except in rooms where everyone is standing

Except in underwater with my grandmother

whose nipples I found when rubbing her stomach

"You must know everything!"

I comefart in secret and feel truly

as if I do.

BLOODTURD, MY FRIEND

bloodturd, my friend

you are ophelia's chinese cousin

and she is also a turd

this stool I stand on has so much meaning

I cry because of the meaning

I cry because of feelings

I find you friendly

exhumed like facing spirits

who give each other

wonderful blowjobs

and that's that

FAIRE CA POUR MOI

my fiscally conservative friend

made me shy

later we chased your mother

she was shy

later we chased your mothers' enceint children

they were ancient

and shy

I was not always so shy

the first sun was your daughter with the malgre tete

we stood there burning

and no one was shy

I was so ferociously shy

I hid my head in the sand

and when they built castles over my stray body

I was just a child

the one you carried home on that very windy day

when you were also

just a child

like me

PHILTER

I'm so nervous you are here the weird world of making play

I'm just so weird you feel like this is play but what have you made

to make me feel so weird you play and I also play

ggggg unngggg unggg ghhhh is the sound of pushing turds

I'm inside of a daisy chain and the lucky Pierre is my boyfriend's penis

inside a whale inside a universe made of fifteen shapes like

round small fixed redundant unapologetic forced queen sand in my eyes

OH, MY BAD

My aubade this morning
before the first blush of a red day
now who was it that said
the universe is ashamed
and who was it that said
the universe is bored
both are true
the universe tells me
and I tell it that we are very much alike
still I serenade the ozone
and the stratosphere
and the hemispheres
and the weird spheres
and the spinning spheres
and the rotating spheres
and the women's spheres
interrupting the men's spheres
overtaking the elderly spheres
reinstating the youthful spheres
which wrinkle and cannot be carried in a tissue
created by this bored universe
this blushing world that has not yet seen me
sing mondegreens
set to my favorite music
"she has incense in her genitals"
but it's incense wine and candles
still in her genitals I take slow sips
I ask to know but not knowing anything
I am told to behave badly
without thinking I know
this August is august.

I'M BAAAAAD

A woman I don't know well
tells me I have a different face
"Did you wear braces before?"
anyone can ask me that
even someone who has seen my face one time
or someone who has seen my face 10,000 times
or someone who was born with my face
or someone who gave birth to my face
or someone who smashed into my face
and thus gave me this face
or someone who told me I had a bad face
thus prompting me to change my face
to give myself this face
which is still a bad face
or just different
this woman thought I looked like anyone
from Sichuan bank in Flushing
where I was not born
where I lived like people live
this woman was my waitress
her friend burped over our food
the last time my mom and I were here
we ate everything and slurped
the remaining liquids
and the remaining sediment
for kidney stones later in life
for fun times in the stony part of life
another time we went to a Korean restaurant
a stinking restaurant smelling as bad
as all the restaurants we go to

the toilets which were holes in the floor
reminded me of the young teenage slam poets
their abuse stories and their refugee stories
and then in class
someone writes about being abused
in a subtle way
that pisses everyone off
especially those who graduated
"summa cum laude"
"You're summa summa something"
I want to say to the universe
"I'm cumma cumma cumming"
he says so loudly that I blush in public
my whole existence prone
to proving things
for the sake of knowing
for the sake of aaa
for the sake of aaaa aaaaa
for the sake of aaaaaa aaaaaaa
for aaaaaaaaaaa aaaaaaaaaaaaa ahwei.

YOU GRANGERIZE

The fifty feeling inside you
became one hundred and no one but me
marveled

In the middle of delivering you across a lawn
feet dragged out like totemic feelings
you considered the possibility:
I feel nothing and you feel everything

I considered the possibility:
You feel everything and I feel everything

Or:
You feel some things and I feel nothing

Or:
I feel nothing and you feel almost everything

Or:
You feel nothing and I feel almost nothing

Either way you are fain
when I offer milk you stomp like a goat
rushing at me like the sheep who trampled my father
because they needed to have
sexy-time

Sexy-time is when you finger the lace that bore my eyes
until everyone in the room yawns big like stone lions

I'm not the stone you sat on

when you pilgrimaged to the holy mountain

where your idols achieved perfect domain

and I laughed cruelly

and felt cruel

and was cruel

and spoke cruel

and danced cruel

and thrashed cruel

You are good like air and have no fears

the offal of yesterday was awful

when birds die in front of my eyes

I feel just as ashamed as the time

I woke you up and said no no no no no

no no no no no no no no no no no no

no no no no no no no no no no no no

no no no no no no no no no no no no

no no no no no no no no no no no no

no no no no no no no no no no no no

no no no no no no no no no no no no

no no no no no no no no no no no no

The whole street heard

I was not ashamed and then I was ashamed

years later your sister learned to joke:

You woke up the whole street, just kidding

Everyone found you loathsome, just kidding

No one sympathized with you, just kidding

They all wanted you to go away, just kidding

I was so ashamed I quit joking
And all my sentences thereafter were too meaningful:
You should eat shit
His horse face is going baa baa baa
My parents' sperm swam like dolphins on my back
I like a man's exposed back and a woman's hidden cunt
Your taint is tainted…

But before I changed there was one more morning

When you woke up to my hovering body
always disappointed I said:
Good morning
the snow outside smells like roses
and I have rubbed their scent over your reposed neck

Right away you glow with no thoughts at all

Why am I in love

FIRST

I was inside of an apple tree growing old

I wrote a poem in Tarascon growing old

I grew old growing old

and being old

I was so utterly enclosed

I closed storied shutters

as an old

I grew old and old and old and old

I had my friends call me

old J and my friends were K or A or B

and I was a cad older than old

I felt good getting old

I was too young to be old

my brother

was not yet born

when I was old

my mother was not yet old

when I grew old

my father was not yet cold

when I was old and watched him like eagles watch frisky clouds separate

in the gulfstream of your infinite love which makes me old

I gather old people

so that I may be among friends

knowing me this old

I long for a long future

those of us with family

leave eaves to hang

and no song to sing at night

I GAVE YOU UNICORN ICE CUBES

I smoked so much
my ears started
singing: 'You will find your prince'
Okay, I found pricey vials
in the virgin forests where virgins are born
knowing everything and like Babel's grandmother
I want to know everything
You must know everything
as a virgin
as someone so completely complete in the infallible first day
when babies were born babies
and virgins born totally good-looking
to insure that ephemeral life was all life and
all life is mine to have
as much as it is not.

I WRITE A MILLION POEMS
A DAY LIKE FRANK O HARA
MULTIPLIED INTO FIFTY FRANK O HARAS

I am also Frank and also so frank with you

on all subjects: the war of peacetime

what your sister ate on the rooftop

the Moroccan sisters who called me in

the prayer of witches in a chadri I sewed

myself in boiling vats like a stomach wanting to be

pierced or thrown like driftwood, your friend Randy

pulled down my pants, first as a joke, and later

you wonder: why's she crying? I am randiest

when you first step into the hallway

I am quiet first and then the rapping is mispelle

French is boring, I revolted only a little

The Catholic church wanted me to be supplicant

and I supplied them with sincere inquiry

Can't I be my own dream? No

you can't and yr tiger laziness is the lioness bounding

well, you have shown de rigeur and the fanfaronade

is yr lowlife for a day, you were born a queen

I eat the squeamish crumby leftovers from your ten greatest feasts

and I feel nothing but lucky, lucky to sleep by yr feet.

VHY DON'T YOU…. TURN YOUR CHILD
AN INFANTA FOR A FANCY-DRESS PARTY?

So I did and this child

returned a succubus

inside the sucking tube

   was me

inside the bus truck

    fifty dead rats

this child in my gold frippery

frip frapped like weirdos

you have so little heart I cave

to your give-in where everyone says

Please give

to the needy (my father)

the poor (your father)

the unloved (my mother)

the pathetic (your mother)

the dead (your grandmother, my grandmother

you in five days or maybe less

or maybe more)

the wha wha wha wha is this

your infanta

    is ugly

so few people worship her and surprise!

I am queen and you lick my feet

just after I declare my need for quiet.

MY BRAIN

I am awake at seven

so what

I was not sleeping through nights

so what

I drank whiskey before I was awake

so what

I ate a hoagie

you think

it's only a finger

I am not worthy

so what

you appear in my dreams

your face as swollen as grapes

I pop your eyes and feel so bad

so what

I wake up shaking

so what

I always wake up shaking

you so what

so what so what so what

I'm not okay

so what

you're worse off so

so you're what

KEY PHASE

That avant guard dood draws so many cunts
I find him weird   he says, yr cute
okay then, cutie
                yr boring me with the cunts
if you would take one cunt out
it would be more cunning than Picasso
but the context is coarse
the hairs are coarse
the 'tude is coarse
I've been coursing through the finite rivers
the smudge of black on yr fingertips and I'm yrs
ya cunt, I'm yrs, yr the cuntiest
cunt I've ever cunted

(I've never heard of Schiele or Matisse)

I scrawled watery touches on the finishing piano
my pinoy boy was all up in yr appropriation
my culture noticed you eat Chinese food

Must save some sharks
ask that whales be spared
pray for suicide jokes
that side split wild mushroom eaters
who became that way
after they were ridiculed on TV
thanks to you for making them think
suicide is what a poet does
in a room when high

The spinning plates became the irises

to a good disease

hydrophrenia: literally

you became retarded in one second

"Yr very girlie!" "Thx."

I'm gurlish and the churly chubbies were in my hands

all five of them left me sane

impeded with farcical farce   can I go

this many days without water or sweating

yes of course I needed this to be yrs

later I'll attack unacceptable fears of being

the imperialist too easy to hate

yr hymn, hmmn, yr him, arentya?

IT WAS GOOD TO DRINK WINE TO PASS TIME BEFORE YOU CAME HOME, I MEAN BAD

What was nice was being drunk

that was nice

you were nice to tell me I was a drunk

I was a drunk

who was very nice

then the window panes were treated

and I treated god's creatures

like precious stones

kicking each one

across shellacked lakes

your fiscal conservatism made me sick

I threw up on netanyahu's pillows

he asked me to do laundry

guess what what

I knew what would happen

and I let it happen anyway

it was frisky and you were fiscal

I feel conservative

and my thighs are not shaking

or feeling conservative

or you are not always inside the globe

where my mail is as male as all made things

I was very lonely and I became non existent

I had almost no dignity

I had nipples that pointed north

and a twat that said hello

when strangers passed in a sweat

I am sweaty waiting for you

always waiting for the mail that comes packed

I am always made and your existence is so wracked

and this is what proves it

the lonely tissue that has no friends

sits beside me with cloud covering

and I contemplate nakedness

beside an old man with no lips

when he talks I hear

yuuuuuuuu aaaaaahhhhhhhuuuuuuuuvvvvvuhh good

and I said good and we're just touching

because of the loneliness I told you about

CHOUETTE

Great, your chou chou has gotten me hard

the soft spots were actually holes where one could put one

finger, that was murder when he filled the hole with fluid

that was murder when he attacked your holes

that was murder when you were just holes and I lived inside both of them

like a para-plume, the military came fuming for me

asked me to figure out water sports

and walked me through old cots, I lived conservatively until

the wanton nudity made me cry.

FUR

The sibylline sylphs who watch over me are so subline in the subalpine air
I breathe with unhappy dignity that I choose to scrape fat cells from my
feet and move with jugal despair

The jovial mothers who were not my mother tried to father me with
sperm collected from the sea

I too see how wrong it is to laugh when fat babies are behaving as badly enceint
fractions

You seem ancient and also new so I dust all windows putting maligned
bullies through pain and the panel panes are also pain au chucka lot I
think of this and I think of you.

I don't want to smoke anymore

I don't want to eat anymore
I don't want to crap anymore
I don't want to wash anymore
I don't want to stumble anymore
I don't want to drive anymore

Then a boy my father's age kisses me
And a boy my brother's age kisses my father
And a boy my brother's father's age kisses my mother
And my mother puts her leg on my leg
And I'm free and anyone can know me

ANYTHING

your tinny hands are inside tins

I grow as I finish fourth

each de grade action is a great thing

I feel like a great thing

great things are called things and this thing is not inside time which is as tinny as

sorry mom

I wasted dishwater again

I feel feelings

this is touchable

Some kids died rollerblading

It's very touchable

my mother spoons me and in kissing my lips she says she wants to stay

like this forever

me too and I also want to be my own mom

and kiss myself

SWAIN

you bird-dog
my date and I saw you
on this curve gentle
lee touching my curve
bikes: my hypocoristic term for you
sample noursing: a bad feeling
the osculation and the reverberation of five chests
the weird fine print of attack
this weird mouth
that won't smile at the nice girls
who won't smile at my nice manners

When she said she was 1/8 Cherokee
I thought/said:
Someone in your family raped a Cherokee
Congratulations
it's okay to be a a a fuc

You should finish lists before leaving for

I have been meaning to

The most wonderful news: I finally

I'm sorry I eve

You

N

JENNY ARE YOU THERE

So if not did you

If did you

If you did did you ask

Ask if you did what

What did you

Did you there or did you

I think if you did

Didn't you ask if

I was there

Then

ON NOT WANTING TO FALL IN LOVE AGAIN

It's December!

Yesterday's trist was tristful

The ice fog that forms in December

Over rocky mountains made of my father's stone feet

He wore ice shoes

Melting over my hyaline face

I wanted to be Proust's little feline cat

These chats I have

Good smiling faces and good smiling acheists.......!

Who make a good living

If I all in love

This is bad

If I wake up with fingers for eyes

Soft cleaning samples with fist-ears

These good years and the long terrible nights

I make you as smart as me

How stupid they were to watch us

The sticky sand dollars and my sticky crying

The cut out fairy in your dairy tales

I finish two cups of trembling

And reach in your direction

The beastly ferns ask me to give up

...Okay then

CAR UNCLE FROSTI

Badly boil   I'm boiling   The greatest bursts and my burst of aaaaaayyyyyyy-
eeeee

These Chinese ladies lead you inside the place where you get 'badfoot
you uhhh her'

who cares if it was supposed to be Sapphic

you ought to dream more   be weird less   o thanks says this one girl
with confidence   no thanks says this other girl with grandiloquence

the grand things about my uncle Frosti is his carbunculars

I said sup?

Suppurating badly, I'm dead moreso than a rotten egg,

Y's before O's,

I need someone to believe in ESL and someone else to invent the undoing of domi-
nance

the stupid tattoo

You hate Chinese people and your arm says 'The guh of my life,' and
having no Chinese friends no one knows to laugh

I'm laughing well at dreadlocks
These apeiro kids keep showing me the endless seas and asking me to
feel small

I feel larger than renamed cities

the old names were an embarrassment

Wanting to date a calligrapher and the dumb snake actually remembered
to eat rocks before vomiting

I learn to swim   the pus spreads and I say, 'This pussy land!'

I PULLED A LEAF FROM MY EYE

It was bothering me for days. Finally I pulled it out, when it was out I put it in my hand, when it was in my hand I put it in my mouth, when it was in my mouth I started to taste it with my tongue, when I tasted it with my tongue I slobbered all over the leaf, when I slobbered all over the leaf I lost my ability to speak, when I lost my ability to speak my father came into my room and asked me two of the most important questions, when he asked me two important questions I tried to overcome my impediment and swallow the leaf, when I tried to overcome my impediment by swallowing the leaf my father got fed up and left me alone in my room, when I was alone in my room I felt the beginnings of pebble pain in my eye, when I began to feel phantom pebbles lodged in my eye I decided to let the leaf slide down my slimy throat, as the leaf was sliding down my slimy throat I suddenly realized I was not a good person, when I had my realization about my character I realized I was crying a lot, when I was crying a lot I felt my tears were hardening into pebbles and the leaves underneath my feet were just the road that led to another road that led to another road that led to the same window I have cried beside since I was born crying in my father's arm with snow on my teeth when it was winter and I had to be handled in every way, and besides, I was not even really alive.

HANS CHRISTIAN

I pulled down his pants

and showed everyone his teeny voice

so high that even the birds shattered—

one shat instead and I felt strong

but I also didn't know who I was

later I felt my heart

it was so slimy we died

it was too sad to think about

so now you wake up and find love in tiny palms

curled like babies

when sleeping alone in cribs

made from oaks your best friends planted

before growing into adults—

I'm also growing

and in the shrubbery of asia

I call myself the swan princess

the orient swells inside me

because of orientalists

I have a name

I walk like the swan's duck cousin walks

Martin Joyce and Kafka

best friends and my best friend

is planting oaks.

MY REAM

In my ream you are small

we're just kids and I cry

telling you anything I cry

in this dream of paper you undevelop

poetry and I still live in dreams

the dream of the paper hallway

which is decorated with sleeves

and the dream of the sleeve where you lived!

I wore fingerless nails

Walter Benjamin reflected like a bague

and my grandfather died in 1940

then my father was born in 1955 and everyone insisted

he was his father's father

I want to go home

I must go home

to chalky floors and your best poetry

moving me like fish move themselves

in the greatest of schools and suddenly

we are no longer a part of this world.

MY MOTHER LEAVES ME A MESSAGE WHERE SHE PRONOUNCES ALL ROMANCE LANGUAGES IN A DEEP VOICE

We are all find she says

bonjour well because

well she is Chinese and anyway

we don't use R's

to think that I will never fall in love

is to be the me I was when I thought

I would never fall in love but I am now

this other me

in love and not too scared

I regret the heart we were captured in

in there I was not a nice person

in there I was a forgetful person

in there I required to know everyone

before anyone can know me

in there no one knew me

in there I was so alone

I might as well have been out there

which is where I am

out here and the deepness of my mother's thoughts

so weighty and impressive

I nearly faint from the love I nearly was capable of.

ACKNOWLEDGEMENTS

"Let them lay their butterflies on a pocket-handkerchief on the gravel" takes its title from *The Waves* by Virginia Woolf.

"Why don't you....Turn your child into an Infanta for a fancy-dress party?" takes its title from Diana Vreeland's monthly column for *Harper's Bazaar*.

"The first fancy feast of fancy" references a line from Kenneth Brower's essay, "The Destruction of Dolphins," for *The Atlantic Monthly*.

Thank you to the editors at *Octopus Magazine* for publishing earlier versions of: "Relish this moment. Hope it will comfort on this raining day," "The Kumiho Inside a Dumb Waiter," and "Let them lay their butterflies on a pocket-handkerchief on the gravel." Thank you to *Weird Deer* for publishing a recording of "Gluing sprinkles on my hangbags."

Thank you to my parents, my brother, and my family in Florida and Shanghai for their love, protection, and resistance.

Thank you to my friends and teachers for the support I did not know I needed until it was already always there. With special thanks to: Vauhini, Sarah, Anna, Karan, Tony, Harry, Ben, Hart, Tom, Esmé, Leslie, Rick, Sam, Connie, Martin, Kyle, Marianne, Claire, Rémy, Hervé, and Cécile.

Thank you to Bruno for sheltering me in his unicorn apartment in Paris.

Thank you to Michael Thomas Taren for encouraging my little art to flower in secret.

Thank you to the Iowa Writers' Workshop for giving me the time and resources to write poetry and seek out adventure.

Thank you especially to Zachary Schomburg, Mathias Svalina, and everyone at Octopus Books for helping me to create something I so violently wanted to create.

JENNY ZHANG *was born in Shanghai and raised in New York. She is a graduate of Stanford University and The Iowa Writers' Workshop.* DEAR JENNY, WE ARE ALL FIND *is her first book.*